MAYFLC

– A Brief History of the Pilgrims and the Mayflower –

MATT NEWBURY

With thanks to...

Nicholas Upton at Southampton City Council, The Mayflower in Rotherhithe, The Harwich Society, Maria Fowler, Alice Pope at Plymouth City Council, Jo Clarke at Plymouth City Council, Plymouth Tourist Information Centre, Sandra Withington at Bassetlaw District Council, Sally Outram at Sally Outram Media, Megan Johnson at Visit Lincoln, Laura Campbell at Dartmouth Mayflower 400, The Fizz Boat, Dartmouth, Tricia Ellis at See Plymouth Massachusetts, Marlijn Kok at Leiden Marketing, Leigh and Sueleen at The Mayflower, Rotherhithe, Aaron Kitts, www.mayflower400uk.org, Wells Newbury de Oliveira and Richard Newbury de Oliveira, Janice Adams, Lorna Reeve and Reverend Jonathan Strickland

Published by Orchard

Orchard is an imprint of Tor Mark,
United Downs Industrial Estate,
Redruth, Cornwall TR16 5HY

www.tormark.co.uk

Published 2020

ISBN 978 1 898964 89 6

ORCHARD

INTRODUCTION

A Remarkable Adventure

"Thus, out of small beginnings greater things have been produced by His hand… and, as one small candle may light a thousand, so the light here kindled hath shone unto many, yea in some sort to our whole nation." Of Plymouth Plantation. William Bradford. Journal written between 1630 and 1651.[1]

The remarkable story of the Pilgrims, their epic voyage across the Atlantic and the founding of the Plymouth Colony is fascinating. While they weren't the first Europeans to discover or indeed colonise America, their story has been passed down over the last four centuries to become the stuff of folk legend. When people in the United States think of their forefathers, they think of those aboard the *Mayflower*, who took the amazingly brave decision to cross the ocean and start a new life in an unfamiliar land.

Refusing to follow the Church of England's teachings, a group of 'Separatists' based around the town of Scrooby in Nottinghamshire began their own breakaway church congregation. After decades of persecution under Elizabeth I and then James I, when they were forced to worship in secret and faced threat of imprisonment and execution, these Separatists led by William Bradford, fled to the Dutch Netherlands. After spending a year in Amsterdam, they relocated to nearby Leiden, where they remained for a further 12 years, able to worship as they pleased under Dutch law.

With the threat of war looming and unable to find decent jobs as non-citizens, the church congregation from Leiden began to make plans to move on again. They were also fearful that their children were becoming too assimilated into Dutch culture and losing their English heritage and religious beliefs. With this in mind, they took the radical decision to settle in Northern Virginia, or New England as it was then known. In August 1620, the group sailed for Southampton, England to meet other colonists who would make the voyage with them.

1 Bradford, W. 1630 – 1631. Of Plymouth Plantation

The plan was to make the crossing to America in two ships, the *Speedwell* and the *Mayflower*. After twice turning back to England because the *Speedwell* leaked, they were forced to leave the second ship in Plymouth. Following a gruelling 66 day voyage the settlers finally reached New England on November 11, 1620. Although the Pilgrims had originally intended to settle near the Hudson River, near the present site of New York City, they were forced to seek shelter at Cape Cod. It was here that the adult men on the ship signed a document we now know as the *Mayflower Compact*, which was to lay the foundation for the community's government. This was later claimed to be the foundation of American democracy.

After exploring the coast to find a suitable place to settle, they discovered what appeared to be an abandoned town that had once belonged to the Wampanoag, a tribe of the indigenous population. It seemed to have everything necessary to build their new home, including a safe harbour, a plentiful water supply, cleared fields and a hillside location with good visibility in all directions. They sailed the *Mayflower* into Plymouth Harbour on 16 December and began building their new settlement. Their first winter was to prove tragically difficult, with the colonists

Plymouth from Mount Batten

falling ill and nearly half of them dying. When the *Mayflower* left to return to England on 5 April 1621, nearly half of the crew had also perished during those first few months.

In the spring, the colonists made contact with the indigenous population and made a peaceful treaty with Ousamequin (also known as Massasoit to the Pilgrims) who was the leader of the Pokanoket Wampanoag tribe. Squanto, a Wampanoag man who had been taken captive by English sailors and lived for a time in London, came to live with the colonists and taught them how to hunt, fish and grow corn. In the Autumn of 1621, the colonists marked their first successful harvest with a three-day celebration and invited Massasoit and 50 of his people to join them in the feast. In the 1800s, this celebration became the basis for the first Thanksgiving.

Following their early trials, the Plymouth Colony began to stabilise and many of the congregation, who had been forced to remain behind in England, journeyed out to join them. Harvests continued to be bountiful and families started growing and by 1627, about 160 were living in the community. It is this extraordinary story of survival that continues to inspire Americans today, especially as so many of them are related to the original settlers. Of the 102 passengers on the *Mayflower*, 24 males produced children to carry on their surnames. Even though half the colony died during their first winter, a staggering 30 million people claim to be their ancestors.

The term *Pilgrim* was coined during the 200th commemoration of the voyage of the *Mayflower*. In William Bradford's account, he describes the passengers on the boat from Leiden as 'saints' and 'pilgrimes'. This book follows the remarkable journey the Pilgrims made from their roots in the villages of North Nottinghamshire, South Yorkshire and Lincolnshire, through their time spent in the Netherlands and then their voyage into New England. It also addresses their relationship with the Native Americans and the catastrophic impact colonisation was to have on the indigenous tribes in the area.

As well as telling the story of the Pilgrims and the *Mayflower*, this book also suggests some of the places that modern Pilgrims may like to visit across the two continents. Many of these sites and visitor experiences were restored and improved for the Mayflower 400 commemorations in 2020, with research and interpretation that debunks some of the more romantic myths and tells the story from a 21st century perspective.

CHAPTER ONE

Pilgrim Roots

England had been a Roman Catholic nation until 1534, when Henry VIII formed the Church of England so he could divorce his first wife, Catherine of Aragon, and marry Anne Boleyn. Religious tensions continued throughout the reign of their daughter, Elizabeth I and through into the reign of James I. Many people felt like the new church retained too many practices of the Roman church and called for a return to a simpler faith and less formal forms of worship. As a result of this desire to live and worship in a purer and more simple form, they became known as 'Puritans'. Meanwhile, a more radical group believed that the Church of England was beyond reform and wanted to set up their own separate church congregations. They were called 'Separatists'.

The Separatists believed that they were true Christians who wanted to 'purify' the Christian church and return to scripture-based services. Their opinions were both radical and illegal in the 1600s and they were driven underground, forced to hold religious services in secret. The Separatist church congregation that would later establish the Plymouth Colony was originally centred around the town of Scrooby in Nottinghamshire. They began meeting in 1606 with members including the young William Bradford and William Brewster.

Monks Mill, Scrooby

By refusing to follow the teachings of the Church of England, the Separatists were viewed as defying the authority of King James I and as such, were traitors. They were harassed, fined and imprisoned for holding meetings and religious ceremonies. After three years of living under constant threat and following several attempts to settle in other parts of England, the group decided to flee to the Netherlands where their religious views would be tolerated.

PLACES TO VISIT
BABWORTH

The first stop on any Pilgrim pilgrimage should be All Saints' Church in Babworth, which dates from the 15th century. It was here that a charismatic preacher; Richard Clyfton, gave sermons that were to prove influential in the foundation of the Separatist movement. William Brewster from Scrooby and William Bradford from Austerfield were regular attendees at these services, walking to the church along the footpath that has since become known as The Pilgrim's Way. Due to his unorthodox views, Clyfton was accused of being non-conformist and removed from his post by the Archbishop's Chancery Court in York. It is thought that following his removal, he set up an underground church at Scrooby Manor in the home of William Brewster, and in doing so, became the spiritual leader of this secret separatist congregation.

Babworth

The entrance to the church is opposite the junction of the A620 and B6420 in a pleasant glade just off the quiet country lane. Park outside and admire

Babworth Church

the small but attractive structure with its tower steeple containing three bells, a clock and a welcoming porch. If the church is open enjoy 19th century stained glass by Kempe, while the chancel and sanctuary contain furniture by Robert (Mousey) Thompson, who was part of the 1920's Arts and Crafts movement. Thompson's trademark carved mice may be seen on several items of furniture. In the early spring the church is surrounded by a magnificent display of snowdrops and a visit to the annual Snowdrop Festival is a real treat.

All Saint's Church, Babworth

The church contains many interesting items recalling the Pilgrims, including the chalice used by Richard Clyfton for his communion services. He escaped to Amsterdam in 1608 and died there on 20 May 1616, while William Brewster and William Bradford both became passengers aboard the *Mayflower*.

The church maintained its links to early American history and heritage when Frank Wilberforce became rector at the start of the 20th century. He was the great grandson of William Wilberforce who led the campaign to abolish slavery.

Robert (Mousey) Thompson carving, Babworth Church

SCROOBY

Scrooby is a small village made up of a handful of delightful buildings on the River Ryton near Bawtry with a population of around 300. However, its cultural significance to millions of Americans cannot be underestimated. Until 1766 the village was on the Great North Road and became a stopping point for many important figures including Elizabeth I and Cardinal Wolsey with the latter staying at Scrooby Manor.

When Separatist preacher Richard Clyfton was stripped of his job at All Saints' Church in Babworth, Scrooby Manor became the secret meeting place for the religious renegades. As they were rejecting the fundamental principles of the state and the established church, there was a real risk of arrest and persecution. Indeed, Brewster and fellow Separatist Richard Jackson were both fined for non-attendance at Scrooby's parish church.[2]

Park at the aptly named Pilgrim Father's Inn (a great place for a pint after your ramble) and cross the road to Church Lane where you will find St. Wilfred's Church, which was known as St James's Church 400 years ago. It was here that leading Mayflower Pilgrim, William Brewster, was almost certainly baptised, as was fellow passenger Susanna White-Windslow. At the north gate to the churchyard you will find the village pinfold, which is now planted with a communal garden. A pinfold is a northern term for a pound which was used to hold stray sheep, pigs and cattle until they were claimed by their owners who would pay a levy or fine for their return. This idea was taken to the English colonies of North America.

Take a stroll along Low Road and you will reach Manor Lane leading to the entrance of Scrooby Manor. The manor was not only home to William and Mary Brewster, but also Susanna White-Winslow, the daughter of Richard Jackson. At the time of their escape to Holland, Jackson was the Bailiff and Receiver and held a lease to the Manor House. Susanna was a key figure in the Pilgrim story, as she was one of three pregnant women to travel on the Mayflower. She gave birth to the first Pilgrim child to be born in the New World, a son called Peregrine. Following the death of her husband William White soon after arriving, her second marriage to Edward Winslow in 1621 was the first English marriage to be conducted in the colony.

2 www.scrooby.net/page/scroobySepereatistChurch accessed by the author 18/2/2020

Scrooby Manor

All that remains of Scrooby Manor is a privately owned cottage, a brick dovecote and the fishponds. They can be seen from a viewing point about 100 metres along Station Road. The rest of the manor house was demolished in the early 19th century, although the levelled area where it stood can still be made out, as well as the twin set of steps (now grassy banks) that lead down to the ornamental ponds. Look out for noticeboards that will tell you the best viewing points. If time allows, visit the nearby market town of Gainsborough (another Puritan stronghold) where there is an Elizabethan manor resembling the one in Scrooby.

Continue walking north along Low Road from Manor Road until reaching Mill Lane which branches off to take you past Monks Mill. This old watermill once formed part of the Scrooby Manor estate. Mill Lane joins the modern Great North Road at a junction opposite Gibbett Hill Lane and then it's just a short stroll back to the Pilgrim Father's Pub.

A brand-new variety of apple was cultivated to mark the 400th anniversary the pioneering voyage of the Mayflower. The 'Pilgrim 400' was planted in towns, cities and villages linking the story of the Separatists with communities; schools and local groups on both sides of the Atlantic were able to apply for a tree to plant. The first of 40 trees was planted at the annual Scrooby Show in the Nottinghamshire village at the heart of the story. The Pilgrim 400 is a round and rosy culinary apple, with creamy white flash and a distinctive sweet flavour. It should grow well in both European and American climates, symbolising the links between the two continents.

AUSTERFIELD

One of the leading Mayflower Pilgrims, William Bradford, was born in the village in the spring of 1590 and was baptised in St Helena's Church. The place of worship is almost 1000 years old and the original font can still be seen today. Remarkably, the font was rediscovered in a farmer's field some 50 years ago. Orphaned at an early age, William was bought up by his uncle, Robert Bradford, who was a churchwarden here. As a teenager, William Bradford became a follower of preacher Richard Clyfton and joined the clandestine Scrooby congregation.

William Bradford would go on to become the second Governor of the Plymouth Colony. To celebrate the importance of the connection, a spectacular stained-glass window was created by Sep Waugh in 1989, for the 400th anniversary of Bradford's baptism. The window depicts William Bradford, the *Mayflower*, the early Plymouth colony and the signing of the *Mayflower Compact*. The window also

St Helena's Church

Mayflower Window, St Helena's Church, Austerfield

features quotes from his famous book, Of Plymouth Plantation: *'we knew that we were Pilgrims,'* and *'one small candle'.* The latter comes from the longer quote, 'Thus out of small beginnings greater things have been produced by His hand that made all things of nothing, and gives being to all things that are; and, as one small candle may light a thousand, so the light here kindled hath shone unto many, yea in some sort to our whole nation.'

Just a short walk northward from the church you will discover Butten Meadow. There are many plaques around the Pilgrim villages commemorating the *Mayflower* passengers, but the one you will find here is particularly tragic. A Delft-tiled plaque commemorates a young member of the congregation called William Butten. He was a young indentured servant of Samuel Fuller, a leader of the church when they travelled to Leiden in Holland. Apparently, the young man was sick for the entire voyage of the *Mayflower* and died within three days of land. He was the only passenger to die out in the open sea, although four more passengers died while anchored off Cape Cod Harbour in November and December 1620. Another memorial near Cape Cod Harbour remembers these five tragic Pilgrims.

Finish your visit with a stroll along to Austerfield Manor House, which was reputedly where William Bradford grew up. It's believed that the impressive manor house may have belonged to Bradford's grandfather and his uncles Robert and Thomas. These wealthy farmers helped raise the orphaned boy who would escape to Holland at the age of 18. In later life this sickly child would become the second elected Governor of Plymouth Colony, a post he held for 30 years. As well as becoming a signatory of the historic *Mayflower Compact*, his journal, 'Of Plimoth Plantation' has provided us with vital details about the historic voyage and the early days of the Colony.

Kings Park, Bassetlaw

THE PILGRIM ROOTS TRAIL

A trail around the Pilgrim Roots area of North Nottinghamshire, Lincolnshire and South Yorkshire has been created by Bassetlaw District Council. It can be downloaded for free at **www.pilgrimroots. co.uk**. A great place to start your tour is at Bassetlaw Museum in Retford where a new gallery was opened as part of the Mayflower 400 Commemorations, celebrating the life of William Brewster, one of the District's most famous sons.

CHAPTER TWO

Escaping to Holland

Guildhall in Boston

With the authorities cracking down the Separatists decided to flee to Holland, a liberal nation where they could live and worship peacefully. One night in the autumn of 1607, they met a boat on the edge of The Wash at Scotia Creek, near Boston in Lincolnshire. Some had walked 60 miles to make their escape under the cover of darkness. However, the captain of a ship betrayed them, and they were captured by the local militia, who stole their money and personal possessions. They were taken back to Boston by boat, where they were held and tried at the Guildhall. Following their conviction, the Separatists were imprisoned for a month.

After their release, the Separatists made a second attempt to leave the country. Choosing the coastal town of Immingham in Lincolnshire for their departure, the Separatists made their escape in 1608. They secured the services of a Dutch boat and her captain to take them to Amsterdam. One of the group, Francis Hawkins, fell ill and his body is buried in the graveyard at St. Andrew's Church. Midway through boarding the ship, men on horseback and others with pistols arrived, looking to arrest them. The ship was forced to set sail with just some of the men onboard, leaving their wives and children behind. Eventually over the coming months, the rest of the congregation (125 in total) were able to reach Amsterdam on other smaller boats.

PLACES TO VISIT
THE BOSTON GUILDHALL COURT ROOM

Guildhall in Boston

Built in the 1390s, visitors can explore the wealth of original features this medieval building has to offer, including the Court Room where the Pilgrims were tried and the basement cells where they were held. There's also a plaque commemorating William Brewster and the Pilgrims. The attraction is open Wednesday through to Saturday and is free to enter. Paid guided tours can also be arranged.

PILGRIM MEMORIAL, SCOTIA CREEK

This memorial at Scotia Creek in Fishtoft marks the place where the Scrooby congregation made their first attempt to flee to Holland. It can be found inside Havenside Countryside Park, on the north bank of the River Haven and was built in 1957 to mark the 350th anniversary of the event. Featuring a small granite obelisk mounted on a granite bloc, it reads "Near this place in September 1607 those later known as the Pilgrim Fathers were thwarted in their first attempt to sail to find religious freedom across the seas." It was erected with donations from the General Society of Mayflower Descendants.

PILGRIM PARK, IMMINGHAM

In Pilgrim Park, Immingham you can visit The Pilgrim Monument which reads "From this creek The Pilgrim Fathers first left England in 1608 in search of religious liberty." It was erected by the Anglo-American Society in 1924 and is made from granite taken from Plymouth Rock in Massachusetts. As the Immingham Dock area expanded the memorial was moved in 1970 to the small park opposite the church. It's fun to try and spot streets that are named after the passengers on the *Mayflower* including Clyfton Crescent, Bradford Road and Brewster Avenue. As well as the Mayflower Pub there's also Pilgrim Academy Primary School. Immingham Museum and Heritage Centre has a small Pilgrim exhibition.

CHAPTER THREE

Going Dutch

When telling the story of the Pilgrims and their gruelling voyage to the New World, it has often been overlooked that this wasn't the first international stop for the congregation of English Separatists. In 1608 they fled to Holland to escape the religious persecution they had endured under the English crown. Initially they moved to Amsterdam which was known for its liberal attitudes, particularly in relation to religious freedom. However, after becoming embroiled in various theological disputes and scandals with other Separatists, the congregation decided to move to Leiden, 25 miles away.

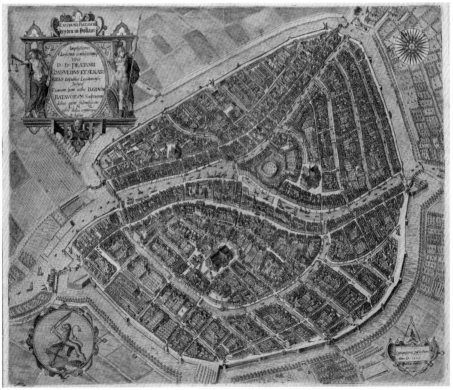

Leiden Map of 1600 by Bast

Leiden in 1601 (at the time of the Pilgrims), by Bast

On the 12th February 1609, the city government of Leiden granted 100 English religious refugees leave to settle in a city known for its free-thinkers, relative religious tolerance and a long tradition of offering shelter to the dispossessed. They would spend twelve years living in exile in the city. Most of the congregation lived in one-room cottages around the Pieterskerkplein Square, under the shadow of one of the oldest churches in the city and a nearby courtyard which become known as Engelse Poort or English Gate. Around half of the congregation took jobs as textile workers, which was the main industry in the city at the time, while others became milliners, pipe makers, carpenters, soldiers and teachers.

It was an interesting time to be living in the city, with botanist Carolus Clusius growing the first European tulips in Leiden's Hortus Botanical Garden and a young Rembrandt attending the Latin School in the same area as the congregation lived. Some of the Pilgrims were also active in public life including John Robinson who took part in theological debates and Thomas Brewster who taught English to Leiden University students. He also arranged for the Pilgrims to be allowed to use one of the university chapels for their services.

There is no doubt that the Pilgrims were influenced by their time in the city and this would prove invaluable in their future lives. As well as the artisan skills they learned through working in Leiden, they also picked up knowledge in terms of legislation, science and acceptance of people from other religions and cultures. Civil marriage was one Dutch innovation they took with them to the New World, while it's widely believed that the origins of Thanksgiving can be traced back to their time spent in the Netherlands. Every year on the third of October, in honour of the celebration of the 1574 Relief of Leiden (the climatic end to the 80-year war for Dutch independence) a celebration takes place, which includes sharing herring and white bread with the local population.

PLACES TO VISIT
THE PILGRIMS ROUTE WALK

The 17th century city of Leiden is a magical place to explore, with 28 km of canals and waterways, 88 bridges, historic buildings and countless 'hofjes' or inner courtyards. And plenty of windmills too! Visit in the spring and you will also find yourself in the centre of the tulip region, while the attractive university city also boasts some great restaurants and bars. The best way to explore the city and to learn more about the Pilgrims is on a city walking tour of Leiden.

Leiden University

Pop into the Tourist Information Centre (Stationsweg 26, close to the main train station) and pick up a copy of the Pilgrims Route self-guided walking tour booklet which allows you to follow in the footsteps of the congregation and their time spent in the city. Highlights include:

PIETERSKERK

The Pieterskerk is a late Gothic church dedicated to St. Peter the patron saint of Leiden. Indeed, the city's symbol is St. Peter's two keys that symbolically unlock the gates to both Heaven and Earth. Boasting almost 900 years of history, the church is associated with the Pilgrims as their leader John Robinson held meetings in his nearby home in the Groene Poort (now Jean Pesijnhof courtyard) and apparently referred to the church's organ as "the Devil's bagpipes". He was too old to travel on the *Mayflower* and is buried inside the impressive church where you will find plaques in memory of him. There's a great café inside, as well as a small Pilgrim's exhibition and a rather wonderful Mayflower Escape Room!

Pieterskerk

Pieterskerk (St Peter's Church) in 1782 by P.Schcuwten

Pieterskerk (St Peter's Church) today

LEIDEN AMERICAN PILGRIM MUSEUM

Knock on the door of this unique museum located in a 14th century house on the charming Beschuitsteeg (Biscuit) Alley. A knowledgeable guide provides information on one of the oldest datable houses in the city with a unique insight into life during the Pilgrims' time. Rather than wandering around reading interpretation, visitors are encouraged to ask questions about the various items in the collection which includes toys, smoking pipes and even a lice comb belonging to a Pilgrim, as well as period furniture, beautiful Delft blue tiles and a selection of historic books and maps. A visit feels more like a fascinating chat, although visitors will leave wondering how a large family could possibly have lived in the one-room home. The Entry ticket also includes access to the adjoining medieval dwelling.

STADHUIS (CITY HALL)

Several of the Pilgrims were married in the truly impressive City Hall and this gave them a familiarity with civil marriage, which they later introduced in their colony. Look out for the gable stone on the front of the building (just to the left of the stairs) which has a poem about the Siege of Leiden engraved on it. The number of letters in the poem corresponds to the 129 days that the siege lasted, while the gold letters are a cryptogram revealing the end date of the siege (1574) in Roman numerals. Do visit the Koornbrug at the rear of the building, where markets are held along the Rhine. Visit at Christmas and a floating market and ice rink are built on the river.

City Hall by Cornelis Springer

City Hall today

YOUNG REMBRANDT STUDIO

A young Rembrandt lived in the city at the same time as the Pilgrims and you will pass the place where he was born (marked with a statue and plaques) on the walking tour, as well as Latin School where he studied. The studio which belonged to Jacob van Langeburgh, under whom Rembrandt also studied, now boasts a gift shop and an impressive audio-visual experience. It tells the story of the first 25 years of the life of Rembrandt, who was to become the most important painter of the Dutch Golden Age. You will also learn of the friendship between the young Rembrandt and Mary Chilton, who according to tradition was the first woman on the *Mayflower* to set foot in America.

WILLIAM BREWSTERSTEEG

During his time in Leiden, William Brewster lived in one of the many 'stinkstegen' (stinking lanes) in the city. They were so called because people would empty their waste into the nearby canals. It is on this lane (called William Brewstersteeg) that Brewster and Thomas Brewer founded a printing shop. They printed and published religious books for sale in England that expressed sentiment in direct conflict with that of the Church of England and James I. The shop was raided and Brewer was arrested, while Brewster fled to Leiderdorp. Brewster could not be prosecuted because he received legal protection under the university where he taught. Brewer was not so fortunate and he was sent back to an English prison where he spent 14 years locked up for his religious beliefs.

DE WAAG

A great place to finish your walking tour is the De Waag (The Weigh House), where the Pilgrims first set foot in Leiden, when their belongings were hoisted ashore at the Waaghoofd. At the spot where the Mare, the Oude Rijn (Old Rhine) and the Nieuwe Rijn (New Rhine) rivers cross, wooden cranes would unload goods from ships before they were weighed to see if any tax was due. At the time The Weigh House would have been built of wood, with the impressive current building built in 1657. Every year on 3 October, herring and white bread are handed out to the local population in celebration of the Relief of Leiden. It was this festival that is said to have inspired Thanksgiving. Today the building houses a bar and restaurant, perfect for some well-earnt refreshments.

Koornbeursbrug in Leiden

CHAPTER FOUR _____
Leaving Leiden

There are various reasons why many of the Pilgrims decided to leave Leiden. Life in the city was difficult both socially and economically, while freedom of press and public debate was also becoming more restrictive. Their stay had also coincided with the Twelve Years' Truce with Spain and war had become a very real threat. The Pilgrims were also concerned that their children were becoming too integrated into the Dutch church and society. Indeed, more than half of the group elected to remain in Leiden and eventually became highly assimilated.

The congregation decided to make the perilous journey across the Atlantic where they hoped to secure true religious freedom by setting up their own settlement. The plan was to leave Holland to set up a farming village in the northern part of the Virginia Colony. At that time, Virginia extended from Jamestown in the south to the mouth of the Hudson River in the north. The Pilgrims planned to settle in an area near what is now New York City. There they hoped to be able to live under the rule of the English government, whilst also enjoying freedom to worship as they pleased.

Galgewater, Stadstimmerwerf, Old Town, Leiden

Without the money to fund this audacious move, they entered into an agreement with financial investors in England. In return for providing tools and clothing supplies and paying their passage, the Pilgrims agreed to send back valuable natural resources, such as fur, timber and fish. All assets, including the land and buildings they would establish the colony with, would belong to the investment company for seven years, before eventually being divided up between the investors and the colonists.

It wasn't possible for all of the Leiden congregation to travel to America at the same time, as they could only secure two ships. As a result, it was agreed an advanced party would be sent, with the others joining them at a later date. A small ship, the *Speewell*, was purchased to carry them across the channel to Southampton where it would meet a larger boat, called the *Mayflower*. From here, the two ships would voyage to Virginia with additional English colonists who had joined at Southampton.

A monument now stands on the spot where the Pilgrims left Leiden on 21 July 1620. Following a final meal and service in the house of Reverend Robinson, 16 men, 11 women and 19 children travelled the 24 miles to Delfshaven near Rotterdam on horseback, by carriage and on foot. They carried all their worldly possessions and were accompanied by many of those who had chosen to remain. In front of the Old Church (now known as the Pilgrim Father's Church) in Delfshaven, John Robinson led the prayers before they said an emotional goodbye to their fellow brethren and friends and boarded the *Speedwell* bound from Southampton. From there the plan was to meet the *Mayflower* and the next step in their incredible adventures.

William Brewstersteeg

Pieterskerk Plaque

CHAPTER FIVE

Harwich and Rotherhithe

HARWICH

The Essex town of Harwich is widely believed to be the home of the *Mayflower*, the ship that famously transported the Pilgrims to the New World. The town is situated on the conflux of the River Stour and River Orwell and has proved a safe natural harbour and an important place in terms of shipbuilding over centuries. During Tudor times in the 1500s, the east coast port was the base for expeditions exploring the world, while it was also home to Christopher Newport, who sailed to America in 1606 and helped build the first English settlement at Jamestown.

The *Mayflower* was constructed around 1590 and while there is no proof she was built in the town, some port documents describe the ship as 'The Mayflower of Harwich' suggesting she possibly was. Also supporting this theory is the fact that her captain and part owner Christopher Jones lived in the town. Somewhat romantically, Jones and his first wife, Sara Twit were neighbours, living across the street from each other. Christopher Jones' former house was restored to a period condition and opened as a museum as part of the Mayflower 400 commemorations in 2020, with a range of bespoke content and interactive elements. Across the other side of Kings Head Street, Sara Twit's former home is now The Alma Inn and Dining Rooms.

Close by is St Nicholas Church where the couple married in 1593. The original church was demolished in 1822 and the

Christopher Jones House

present one built on the site. The romantic story takes a sad turn, as the church was also the place where their son was baptised and then buried after he died in infancy. Sara also died aged just 27. Christopher remarried in the same church soon after and had 8 children with his second wife, Josian. In

Harwich

1611 Christopher Jones is recorded as moving to the Rotherhithe parish (then in Surrey, now in London) where he lived till his death in 1622.

Harwich is also believed to be the hometown of at least three other *Mayflower* passengers. The ship's pilot, Robert Coppin, may have been one of the Copping family of Harwich, while Richard Gardener was a seaman who was baptised in Harwich in 1582. He was a part owner of the *Mayflower*, who returned with the ship to England after the voyage. Finally, John Alden was a cooper who looked after the barrels of food and water aboard the ship – a vital role. He was recruited when he was about 21 years old in Southampton and chose to stay in America where he became one of the main builders of the early colonies.

A brand-new Heritage Centre opened to coincide with the Mayflower 2020 celebrations, with a dedicated exhibition exploring the town's role in the *Mayflower*'s journey. It includes artefacts that have never been publicly displayed before. An informative way to explore the town is to follow the Maritime Heritage Trail, which can be downloaded for free. It takes in all of the sites mentioned above, as well as the Ha'penny Pier and Visitor's Centre, from where the Harwich Society offers free guided walks every Saturday between May and September (**www.harwich-society.co.uk**).

ROTHERHITHE

London played a central role in the story of the voyage of the *Mayflower*. Many of the passengers lived in the city and worshipped in St Saviour's (now Southwark Cathedral) and St George the Martyr Churches in Borough. The Separatists raised the money they needed through the Merchant Adventurers of London, a trading company which saw a market for opening up trade routes with the New World. The merchants agreed to finance the settlers' trip in return for repayment of their expenses and added interest from any profits made. The Separatists would have negotiated with the investors and with James I (to secure their freedom to leave) in Heneage House, which is now the site of Bevis Marks Synagogue and Ironmongers Hall.

Mayflower Pub, Rotherhithe

Some 65 passengers would have boarded the *Mayflower* from its homeport of Rotherhithe on the River Thames. It's been suggested that the Captain, Christopher Jones, cunningly moored here to avoid paying taxes further down the river. Somewhat conveniently, the original mooring point of the *Mayflower* can be spotted from The Mayflower Pub, which is the oldest pub on the river. It's a must-visit for anyone exploring the history of the Pilgrims – or indeed anyone who just fancies a cheeky pint. The historic hostelry stands where The Shippe Pub was in the 16th century and was given its current name in 1957 to mark its connection to the colonists.

The Mayflower Descendants Book is available upon request to those who can prove a family connection to the original Pilgrims, and you are invited to share your details and sign the book. You may also want to write a postcard while you are there, as they are the only pub in the UK licensed to sell UK and US postage stamps. This tradition dates back to the 1800s (when the pub was called The Spread Eagle) when seafarers docking at Rotherhithe could save time by ordering a pint and buying their stamps at the same time.

The captain of the *Mayflower*, Christopher Jones, moved to Rotherhithe in 1611. He would return to London on the *Mayflower*, arriving back in Rotherhithe on 6 May 1621. Exhausted from the hardships he endured, he died less than a year later and was buried at St. Mary's Church. There is a blue plaque on the side of the church, as well as a memorial statue sculpted by Jamie Sargeant in 1995. A stylised figure of St Christopher looks back to the Old World, while a child in his arms looks forward to its future in the new.

CHAPTER SIX

Southampton and Dartmouth

SOUTHAMPTON

The *Mayflower* departed from London in the middle of July 1620 and sailed down to Southampton to meet the *Speedwell*, which was carrying the Leiden Separatists from Holland. The two ships planned to make the transatlantic voyage together, but there were issues with the *Speedwell*, which had developed a leak and required repairs. One theory is that the boat, which was possibly built in Southampton in 1606, had too large a mast and sail area.

As a thriving seaport, with established trading links with Newfoundland and Virginia, there was an experienced pool of seamen in the town. John Alden, a cooper, joined the *Mayflower* here, while it's likely that William Brewster also slipped aboard, having been in hiding since publishing material that had angered King James. Stephen Hopkins also joined the crew here, famed for being the only *Mayflower* passenger with previous experience of the New World, having been shipwrecked in Bermuda 11 years earlier.

Southampton was also an ideal place to shop for provisions to set up their new community across the Atlantic. There were merchants selling the supplies necessary for such an expedition and indeed many of the streets and buildings that the Pilgrims would have grown familiar with still exist. Once repairs had been made to the *Speedwell*, the two ships set sail on 15 August 2020.

West Gate

The Pilgrims would have left through the Westgate, which led through the old city walls and onto the West Quay where the boats were waiting. Much of the medieval city walls are still intact, as is the gate

City wall, Southampton

Holy Rood Church, Southampton

tower, which has a plaque commemorating not only the Pilgrims, but the soldiers of Henry V who also passed through here on their way to Agincourt in 1415. The gate is close to Pilgrim Park, where you will find the Grade II listed Mayflower Memorial, which was designed by RM Lucas and unveiled in 1913. On top of the 50-foot-high column of Portland stone is a cupola and copper model of the *Mayflower*. The memorial was restored as part of the Mayflower 400 commemorations in 2020.

The city is proud of its association with the Pilgrims, with The Mayflower Theatre, the Mayflower Cruise Terminal and even university accommodation called Mayflower Halls. It's worth booking yourself onto a walking tour to learn more about Southampton's nautical heritage that takes in everything from Viking invasions to the sailing of the *Titanic*. The Tudor House Museum and the Medieval Merchants House are also worth a visit.

DARTMOUTH

Soon into the voyage, the *Speedwell* still taking on water, the crew were forced to put into Dartmouth for further repairs. The leaks may have been caused by the ship carrying too much sail, straining her timbers or possibly something more sinister. There have been rumours across the centuries that Master Reynolds, the captain of the *Speedwell* was afraid either of the Atlantic crossing or of starving to death in the new colony and purposely made the leaks himself. It is also possible the leaks were caused by a reluctant crew. With the *Speedwell* sinking, the two ships were forced to pull into the Devonshire town of Dartmouth for repairs.

The repairs were made in Bayard's Cove harbour, with the *Mayflower* moored upstream at what is now known as Pilgrim Hill. While the waterfront has changed over the years, Dartmouth retains many historic buildings the Pilgrims would recognise. These include the Tudor Bayard's Cove Fort, Lower Street, Smith Street, St Saviour's Church and Agincourt House, which is now the Bayard's Cove Inn. The best way of exploring these sites is to follow the Mayflower Heritage Trail, which was created for the Mayflower commemorations in 2020.

The trail route is based on a map of the town drawn in 1619 and paints a colourful picture of the historic town in the 17th Century. Pick up a trail map from either the Visitor Centre or Dartmouth Museum and follow the route around the historic streets, where you will find interpretation panels at key locations. It's beautifully put together and not only takes in the *Mayflower* story but the rich history of the naval town itself. A new sculpture was also commissioned for the 400-year anniversary of the voyage, representing a Pilgrim looking out to sea. It was created by artist Mark Gregory with the help of pupils from Dartmouth Academy. It's situated on the South Embankment.

The two ships arrived in Dartmouth on the 23 August 1620 and it took almost a week for the port's skilled boatbuilders to repair the *Speedwell*. The two boats headed out of the mouth of the River Dart and into the English Channel on about August 31 with some 122 people on board. Unfortunately, when the ships were 200 miles beyond Land's End, the *Speedwell* sprang a further leak and both ships were forced to turn back for Plymouth, less than 156 nautical miles from Southampton.

Mark Gregory sculpture, Dartmouth

CHAPTER SEVEN

Plymouth

By the time the *Mayflower* and *Speedwell* arrived in Plymouth, provisions were low and the passengers were damp and worn out, having been in cramped conditions for more than a month. They were still on the south coast of England, when they should have been close to their final destination by now. The *Speedwell*

Plymouth, Devon

was finally declared unfit for the journey and it was decided that the *Mayflower* would continue alone. Some of the Pilgrims dropped out at this point, with the remainder crowding onto the one boat. The ship required more provisions, despite funds running seriously low.

In spite of all of the obstacles, she left on 16 September 1629 with 102 passengers and 30 crew on board. Of the passengers, 50 were men, 19 women and 33 were young adults or children. By this point, just 41 were religious Separatists escaping the religious confines of the Church of England. The others were considered common folk that the Pilgrims called the "strangers" and included merchants and craftsmen, as well as indentured servants and orphaned children.

By a quirk of fate, Plymouth became the final place that the *Mayflower* set off from and this unique honour led to a year-long programme of events in 2020. The Mayflower Trail was also created by Visit Plymouth and is a great way of exploring the Barbican and Hoe areas of the city. The walk can be downloaded for free from (**www.visitplymouth.co.uk**).

PLACES TO VISIT
THE MAYFLOWER MUSEUM

Located above the Tourist Information Centre and built over three floors, this is an ideal place to begin your explorations. After stepping out on the upstairs balcony to take in panoramic views over the Barbican, visitors can enjoy various exhibits related to the Pilgrims. A highlight is the model of the *Mayflower*, built by apprentices from Devonport Royal Dockyard for the 150th anniversary of the sailing.

THE ISLAND HOUSE

This building is believed to have been one of several in which the Pilgrims lodged before their departure for the New World. Today the building is home to the Pilgrim Ice-Cream Parlour, and you will of course need to sample the treats on offer. There are two plaques on the walls of the building, one listing those who sailed aboard the *Mayflower*.

NEW STREET AND THE ELIZABETHAN HOUSE

Elizabethan House, Plymouth

This area of Plymouth allows you to step back in time to what the city would have looked like in the time of the Pilgrims, although don't let the name New Street deceive you. It was built between 1575 and 1600, so is actually a very old street. The cobbles will take you to a row of former merchant houses along this street dating back to the 1500s, with no. 32 being the home to a former sea-captain. It's now a museum and was restored for the Mayflower 400 commemorations.

THE ELIZABETHAN GARDENS

These nearby gardens are a delightful oasis created in a space left empty after the slum clearances in the 1920s and 1930s. Bricks were taken from nearby buildings that were bomb damaged in the Second World War and a knot garden was created. You will also discover a memorial to the Pilgrims and a stone carving of the *Mayflower*.

Elizabethan Gardens, Plymouth

THE BLACK FRIARS PLYMOUTH GIN DISTILLERY

This impressive medieval building is one of the oldest surviving structures in Plymouth, dating back to 1431. It's believed that the site was a former home to a Dominican Order Monastery and the upstairs bar (now called The Refectory) is said to be where the Pilgrims spent their last night before sailing. In 1793 the building was converted into a distillery producing Plymouth Gin, making it the oldest working gin distillery in the UK. As part of the packaging there is a thirsty monk printed inside the bottle and it is said that when the monk's feet 'got dry' it was time to get a new bottle. The label on the front also depicts the *Mayflower* and another suggestion is that one should buy a new bottle when the *Mayflower* 'no longer sails on gin.' Tours can be booked with samples included.

Plymouth Gin

THE NEW CUSTOM HOUSE AND OLD CUSTOM HOUSE

Built over a number of years, partly by French prisoners of war, the New Custom House was completed in 1820 and was occupied by the Excise for 190 years. Originally it would have included stables and a Queen's Warehouse, where seized goods could be destroyed. Today it is home to a wedding and events venue and a stylish hideaway bar. The Old Customs House (found opposite the new one) dates back to the late 1500s and it is believed the Pilgrims would have needed to be checked in here with their documentation when they were forced to transfer the contents of the two ships onto one. The building was later used as a barracks and today it houses the Book Cupboard bookshop.

JACKA BAKERY

This is the UK's oldest commercial working bakery which dates back to 1597. It's claimed that the bakery supplied ships biscuits for the *Mayflower* voyage, and it's definitely worth popping in for supplies today. It's been voted the best bakery in the UK.

THE MAYFLOWER STEPS

The Mayflower Steps were built in Sutton Harbour in 1934, close to the spot where the *Mayflower* departed. However, according to local legend, the original steps are actually under the women's toilets of the nearby Admiral MacBride pub. The theory is the pub was built on top of the steps some 300 years ago. The hostelry receives large numbers of visitors on the back of this urban legend.

Lookout point above the Mayflower Steps, Plymouth

Mayflower Steps, Plymouth

Jacka Bakery, Plymouth

CHAPTER EIGHT _____
Life on Board

The *Mayflower* set sail from Plymouth on September 6, 1620 on what Bradford called a "prosperous wind". While Plymouth is traditionally regarded as the last stop of the *Mayflower* before she made the transatlantic voyage, the people of Newlyn in Cornwall would beg to differ. A plaque in the fishing port states: "To the memory of Bill Best Harris 1914 – 1987 Historian and son of Plymouth whose researches indicated that the MAYFLOWER 16-8-1620 docked at the Old Quay Newlyn for water and supplies making it the last port of call in England the water supply at Plymouth being the cause of fever and cholera in the city. Let debate begin." It's a tantalising theory, although sadly the evidence was lost in a fire and the historian in no longer alive to provide any proof.

The main source of what we know about life on board comes from the first-hand account of William Bradford, who went on to become the second governor of the colony. In later years he wrote a journal called 'Of Plimoth Plantation' which is an invaluable source of information. We are very lucky to still have this manuscript, as it was lost in the American War of Independence. He makes no reference to the Newlyn stop, but does describe how the early days of the voyage were smooth, although there was quite a lot of sea sickness. However, shortly after life took a turn for the worse, as he explains:

"After they had injoyed faire winds and weather for a season, they were incountred many times with crosse winds, and mette with many feirce stormes, with which y shipe was shroudly shaken, and her upper works made very leakie; and one of the maine beames in y midd ships was bowed & craked, which put them in some fear that y shipe could not be able to performe y vioage."

In an age when an aeroplane can get you to America in six or seven hours and a cruise ship in six or seven days, it's hard to imagine what life must have been like for the 102 people who spent 66 days aboard in cramped conditions. The *Mayflower* was not a large ship, just 100 feet long weighing 180 tons. It was built to transport cargo not people and the passengers were crowded below decks, hanging curtains for privacy. They slept when they could, on wooden pallets attached to the walls, on hammocks made from cloth or simply on the bare floor. They shared the space with live animals including sheep, goats and poultry, as well as at least two dogs – a spaniel and an English mastiff.

As well as the passengers, the ship was also carrying everything needed to set up the colony, with the decks stacked floor to ceiling with tables, beds, rugs, chairs, chests of clothes, shoes, pillows, tools, dishes and seeds to plant. There were also large barrels containing food and drink. Passengers would have eaten dried meat and fish, boiled cabbage, sea biscuits called hardtack, dried fruit and cheese and all washed down with beer, which was much safer to drink than the water.

In between the monotony, there was also a fair share of drama. William Burton, a servant of Samuel Fuller, is the only passenger to die during the voyage. He would have been buried at sea. Meanwhile Elizabeth Hopkins, wife of Stephen Hopkins, gave birth to a son, Oceanus Hopkins, during the voyage. A young man called John Howland was also knocked overboard during a violent storm and only survived when he managed to grab onto a topsail halyard that was trailing in the water. Remarkably, passengers were able to haul him back on board. Howland and his eventual wife Elizabeth Tilley, (another *Mayflower* passenger) went on to have 10 children and more than 80 grandchildren. An estimated two million Americans can trace their roots to him and if he hadn't survived, ancestors including Franklin D Roosevelt, George HW Bush and George W Bush, Christopher Lloyd, Humphrey Bogart, Sara Palin, Anthony Perkins and Chevy Chase, Dr Benjamin Spock and Mormon church founder Joseph Smith would never have existed.[3]

Cramped conditions, sickness and rough seas would have made the voyage almost unbearable. There were also conflicts on board, with the Pilgrims trying to impose their beliefs on the shipmates, who in turn would swear and treat the passengers with contempt. With tensions at breaking point, the two groups realised that cooperation was the only way they could survive both the voyage and life in the New World. The male passengers held an emergency meeting and created the *Mayflower Compact*, an agreement that served as the basis for their future legal and social organisation. It became the first governing document of the Plymouth Colony and the forerunner of the Constitution of the United States of America.

3 https://pilgrimjohnhowlandsociety.org/Notable_Howland_Descendants accessed by the author 18/02/2020

CHAPTER NINE

Arrival

After 66 arduous days at sea, the crew sighted land at what is now Cape Cod. When they left England, the Pilgrims had obtained permission from the King to settle on land near the mouth of the Hudson River at what is now New York However, when they tried to sail down the coast, strong winds forced them back into the harbour at Cape Cod, where they anchored on 21 November, months after their planned arrival date. Shortly after, Susannah White gave birth to a son aboard the *Mayflower*, the first English child to be born in the colony. He was named Peregrine, which is derived from the Latin for 'Pilgrim'.

On 27 November, the ship's captain, Christopher Jones, 24 passengers and 10 sailors went on a reconnoitre to find a suitable site for settlement. They went to shore in the smaller shallop that had been carried on the *Mayflower*. They were ill-prepared for the winter weather with its below-freezing temperatures, going ashore in wet shoes and stockings that soon became frozen. They spent a night ashore due to the bad weather and Bradford wrote in his account that[4] "Some of our people that are dead took the original of their death here" on that expedition.

The Pilgrims spent the next six weeks exploring the coastline, while most of the passengers remained on board where they felt safer and warmer over the winter months. Myles Standish, who had been hired by the Pilgrims to be their military captain and coordinate the Colony's defence, led the exploration. They were being watched by a small group of Native Americans who were understandably suspicious of the new arrivals. On sighting them, the colonists tried to follow the natives, but got lost and stuck in dense thickets. On trying to find their way back to the ship, they stumbled upon an area of cleared land with abandoned houses. They also found graves.

They had stumbled upon a village called Patuxet, that had been deserted following the outbreak of disease. The curious settlers dug up some mounds that they found and discovered that some stored corn and others that were burial sites. According the Bradford's account, the Pilgrims took some of the corn intending

4 https://www.mayflower400uk.org/education/who-were-the-pilgrims/2019/november/the-mayflower-compact-the-first-governing-document-of-plymouth-colony/ accessed by the author 18/02/2020

to plant it and grow more, eventually planning to return what they had taken. He says:

"Also there was found more of their corn and of their beans of various colours; the corn and beans they brought away, purposing to give them full satisfaction when they should meet with any of them as, about some six months afterward they did, to their good content."[5]

Of Plymouth Plantation. 1620 – 1647. William Bradford.

The Native Americans in the region were from various groups of the Wampanoag people and other tribes, who had lived there for 10,000 years before the English arrived. European diseases were just one of the devastating legacies of the colonisation of the Americas. Ships from England had been fishing and trading in these waters since the beginning of the 16th century. European explorers also brought back Native Americans, some of whom became slaves and were cruelly exhibited at attractions and fairs.

Others were taught English, so they could act as interpreters. In 1614 (six years before the arrival of the Pilgrims), 27 Native Americans were seized by a man called Thomas Hunt. The majority of these people came from Patuxet, the very village the Pilgrims had stumbled upon. One of these villagers was called Tisquantum (also known as Squanto). Hunt tried to sell the natives as slaves in Spain but somehow Tisquantum made his way to England. Here he learned some English and remarkably was used as an interpreter on future trips to America. Tragically when he finally found his way back to Patuxet, he found that his family and the rest of the villagers had been wiped out by disease bought by European settlers and explorers. Between 1616 and 1619, a mysterious disease that would be known as the 'Great Dying' ravaged the region, wiping out whole villages, meaning the *Mayflower* passengers had arrived in a place that had already suffered terribly from colonisation.

Before deciding to build their colony on what is now Plymouth, the Pilgrims explored other areas down the coast, including an area inhabited by the Nauset people. They saw some of the tribe on the shore, but they fled when they were approached. They also discovered more burial mounds which they decided not to dig. They remained ashore overnight and the following morning were attacked with arrows. They retaliated with guns but could not find their attackers. This was the last contact until the following spring.

5   Bradford, W. 1630 – 1631. Of Plymouth Plantation

PLACES TO VISIT
THE PILGRIM MONUMENT

Visiting Provincetown, it's impossible to miss the 252-foot Pilgrim Monument, that commemorates their first landfall in America. President Theodore Roosevelt sailed into the harbour on his yacht, the USS *Mayflower* to lay the cornerstone in 1907. The ornate Italianate tower (modelled after one in Siena, Italy) was completed in 1910 and remains the tallest all-granite structure in the U.S. Visitors may climb the 116 steps for a breath-taking 360-degree panoramic view of Cape Cod Bay. Each November, 3000-plus 'landing lights' illuminate the monument and shine for five weeks, which was roughly the amount of time the Pilgrims spent in Provincetown. There is a museum at the base of the monument, with a history of the town as well as exhibits relating to the Pilgrims.

FIRST LANDING PARK

This small park with a strangely discreet plaque marks the place where the Pilgrims first set foot on land. This is known with some certainty thanks to a booklet called *Mourt's Relation*, which was predominently written by Edward Windslow, who would become the third Governor of Plymouth Colony. The publication includes a map that shows the spot where they first landed.

CORNHILL

Cornhill is located in Barnstable County, Massachusetts and it is here that the Pilgrims are believed to have discovered and taken much of a store of corn. Sixteen of the settlers, led by Miles Standish, William Bradford, Stephen Hopkins and Edward Tilley came ashore at the mouth of the Pamet River and climbed a nearby hill where they discovered the Payomet Indian's winter store of corn. That spot, now marked by a small monument, lies just over 100 feet from the entrance to Corn Hill Landing.

FIRST ENCOUNTER BEACH

This beach is in Eastham in Barnstable County and as the name suggests, it marks the location of the first encounter between the Pilgrims and the Native Americans. While exploring the coast of Cape Cod Bay, Captain Myles Standish and his party camped here. They were disturbed by a group of Nausets and shots were fired. A memorial on the knoll on the north end of the beach marks the spot of the encounter.

Pilgrim Monument, Provincetown MA

CHAPTER TEN

The Plymouth Colony

Following the skirmish, the Pilgrims decided to find another area to make their new home and on December 25, 1620 the *Mayflower* departed Provincetown and sailed into what is now Plymouth Bay, Massachusetts. Here they began the construction of their first buildings. During that first harsh winter, the passengers remained on board the *Mayflower*, where a contagious disease described as a cross between scurvy, pneumonia and tuberculosis broke out. By the time it had ended, over half the passengers and crew had died.

The settlement's first structures to be built were a fort and a watchtower, on what is now known at Burial Hill. It was named as the area contains the graves of Bradford and other original settlers. The first house was built to be a hospital, with only 47 of the colonists still alive after the first winter. With over half of the *Mayflower* crew dead, Coles Hill was used as the first cemetery, overlooking the beach.

Each single man was assigned to live with one of the 19 families, reducing the need to build any more structures than necessary. Each of the extended families was given a plot to build their house on, with most of the settlement constructed by February. This is a remarkable feat, with only six or seven of the colonists well enough to build, as well as feed and care for the others. When his remaining crew were well enough, Christopher Jones sailed the *Mayflower* back to England, taking half the time it did on the way out.

The land at Plymouth where the Pilgrims had decided to settle was home to the Wampanoag tribe who had hunted, fished and harvested in the region for 10,000 years. Following the Great Dying and the devastating losses, various tribal chiefs, known as Sachems, had joined together to build new unions. During March 1621 an English-speaking member of the Wamponaog named Samoset entered the Plymouth colony and introduced himself. He is said to have asked for a beer and spent the night talking with the settlers.[6]

6 https://www.mayflower400uk.org/about/brief-history-of-the-mayflower/ accessed by the author 18/02/2020

Samoset brought another member of his tribe called Tisquantum to meet them. As his English was more advanced, he taught the settlers where to plant corn, fish and hunt for beaver. He also introduced them to the Wampanoag chief, Ousamequin, and the chief of the Pokanoket people, Massasoit. Edward Windslow, an experienced diplomat and one of the men who signed the *Mayflower Compact* handled negotiations towards a peace treaty.

The Wampanoag tribe were cautious of the nearby Narragansett tribe, who had not been affected by The Great Dying. As a powerful tribe they were insisting that the Wampanoag people show them honour and tribute. Ousamequin would have realised that an alliance with the colonists would help fend off any attacks from the rival tribe. Indeed, when the Narragansett sent a warning to the settlers in the form of arrows wrapped in snakeskin, Bradford replaced the arrows with bullets and sent the skins back. The tactic worked.

The peace treaty proved a great success, with the two groups sharing skills and knowledge. The Wampanoag taught the settlers how to hunt, farm and get the best from their harvest, which almost certainly saved them from starvation. The friendship between the two nations saw Winslow helping nurse Ousamequin back to health when he fell ill, by feeding him a special chicken soup. Such was the strength of the relationship; they would end up sharing the first Thanksgiving together.[7]

PLACES TO VISIT
PLYMOUTH ROCK

Plymouth Rock & Portico, Plymouth MA

More than a million people visit this boulder, which according to legend is where the Pilgrims landed in 1620. Although there is no historical evidence to confirm this was the stepping stone, it was identified as the spot in 1741 – 121 years after the arrival of the *Mayflower*. A 94-year old church elder called Thomas Faunce, said that his father (who arrived in 1623 with some of the original *Mayflower* passengers) told him it was. Regardless of its authenticity, it has become a powerful symbol in American history and 1620 was carved into the rock in 1880.

7 https://www.mayflower400uk.org/education/the-mayflower-story/ accessed by the author 18/02/20

Plymouth Hall Museum

PILGRIM HALL MUSEUM

The nation's oldest continuously operating public museum houses an incredible collection of Pilgrim possessions that really bring the story to life. See William Bradford's Bible, Myles Standish's sword, the only portrait of a Pilgrim (Edward Winslow) painted from life, the cradle of New England's first–born, Peregrine White, the great chair of William Brewster, and the earliest sampler made in America, embroidered by Myles Standish's daughter. You will also learn the story of the Wampanoag, 'People of the Dawn', and the impact the settlers would have upon their lives.

Plimoth Plantation

PLIMOTH PLANTATION

A living history museum that recreated life at the time of the immigrants. See reenactors demonstrate blacksmithing, farming and cooking all while dressed in period costume. The re-creations are based upon a wide variety of first-hand and second-hand records, accounts, articles, and period paintings and artefacts. The site also includes a *Mayflower* II replica (see below) and the Wampanoag Homesite where Native Americans from a variety of tribes and in traditional costume explain and demonstrate how the Wampanoag's ancestors lived and interacted with the settlers.

The Mayflower II

THE MAYFLOWER II

This faithful replica was built in Brixham, Devon between 1955 and 1956 using traditional methods. It sailed from Plymouth in Devon on 20 April 1957 recreating the original voyage, arriving in Plymouth Massachusetts on June 22. It was then towed up the East River into New York City where the crew received a ticker-tape parade. The ship represents the alliance between the United Kingdom and the United States for collaboration during the Second World War. The ship spent five years being restored in Mystic, Connecticut, before returning to Plimoth Plantation permanently for the Mayflower 400 commemorations.

ALDEN HOUSE HISTORIC SITE

John Alden and Priscilla Mullins arrived in Plymouth Colony on the *Mayflower* in 1620 and were married about 1622. In 1627, they moved to live in this house, now a visitor attraction, where they raised their 10 children. Immortalised in Henry Wadsworth Longfellow's 1858 poem, *The Courtship of Miles Standish*, their love story is one of the first romances in the colony. Standish, "a blunt old captain" took a liking to Mullins "the loveliest maiden of Plymouth." Although fearless in battle, he was too shy to approach her, so he sent his young friend, John Alden, to plead his case. The couple found themselves unavoidably attracted to each other but were afraid of offending the Captain. However, when they received word he had died in battle, they agreed to marry. At the end of the wedding, Standish, who had not died, returned. On seeing their happiness, he gave the newlyweds his blessing and asked forgiveness for his previous behaviour.

LEYDEN STREET AND COLES HILL

Take an historic walking tour of Leyden Street, the site of the original Pilgrim settlement and the oldest continuously inhabited street in the U.S. Nearby, Coles Hill was used as a burial ground during their first winter and there are a number of monuments and memorials, most dating from the 300-year anniversary. These include a statue of the Wampanoag sachem Massasoit, whose support was critical to the settlers' survival. There is also a granite sarcophagus that contains skeletal remains accidentally disinterred from the hill in the 18th and 19th centuries, which are believed to be those of *Mayflower* settlers buried here in the winter of 1620-21 when 52 out of 102 Pilgrims died.

Coles Hill Sarcophagus & Massasoit overlooking Plymouth rock, Plymouth MA

CHAPTER ELEVEN

The First Thanksgiving

Following a bumper harvest in the autumn of 1621, the colonists decided to celebrate with a thee-day festival of prayer. In attendance were 90 Native Americans and the 53 Pilgrims. The exact date of the celebration is unknown although experts suggest it was likely to be around Michaelmas on 29 September. A feast was cooked by the four adult Pilgrim women who had survived the first winter – Eleanor Billington, Elizabeth Hopkins, Mary Brewster and Susanna White. They would have been assisted by the younger women and both male and female servants.

There are two detailed accounts of the celebration, written by William Bradford and Edward Winslow:

"They began now to gather in the small harvest they had, and to fit up their houses and dwellings against winter, being all well recovered in health and strength and had all things in good plenty. For as some were thus employed in affairs abroad, others were exercised in fishing, about cod and bass and other fish, of which they took good store, of which every family had their portion. All the summer there was no want; and now began to come in store of fowl, as winter approached, of which this place did abound when they can be used (but afterward decreased by degrees). And besides waterfowl there was great store of wild turkeys, of which they took many, besides venison, etc. Besides, they had about a peck a meal a week to a person, or now since harvest, Indian corn to the proportion. Which made many afterwards write so largely of their plenty here to their friends in England, which were not feigned but true reports."[8]

Of Plymouth Plantation. 1620 – 1647. William Bradford.

"Our harvest being gotten in, our governor sent four men on fowling, that so we might after a special manner rejoice together after we had gathered the fruits of our labor. They four in one day killed as much fowl as, with a little help beside, served the company almost a week. At which time, amongst other recreations, we exercised our arms, many of the Indians coming amongst us, and among the rest their greatest king Massasoit, with some ninety men, whom for three days we entertained and feasted, and they went out and killed five deer, which we brought to the plantation and bestowed on our governor, and upon the captain and others. And although it be not always so plentiful as it was at this time with us, yet by the goodness of God, we are so far from want that we often wish you partakers of our plenty."[9]

Mourt's Relation: A Journal of the Pilgrims at Plymouth, 1622, Edward Winslow.

Although many Americans regard this as the first Thanksgiving, the *Mayflower* and the Pilgrims' settlement was largely forgotten until Bradford's journal was rediscovered in England in the 19th century. With a liberal depiction of colonists, their story was used in the years preceding the Civil War to show how the colonists in the north were far more tolerant and moral than those in Jamestown, Virginia who had preceded them. Lincoln seized upon the Pilgrims' story and their values of equality and freedom in his position on the Civil War. He contrasted the spirit of the *Mayflower* with that of the 'other' America, the south, which was backward, intolerant and built on slavery. In 1863, while the battle was still raging, he made Thanksgiving an annual national holiday. It was thanks to Lincoln's victory two years later that it is the Pilgrims' story that continues to dominate the history books.

President John F. Kennedy issued Proclamation 3560 on November 5, 1963 stating, "Over three centuries ago, our forefathers in Virginia and in Massachusetts, far from home in a lonely wilderness, set aside a time of thanksgiving. On the appointed day, they gave reverent thanks for their safety, for the health of their children, for the fertility of their fields, for the love which bound them together and for the faith which united them with their God."[10]

The Native American activist group, The United American Indians of New England, continues to raise awareness of racism and the consequences of colonialism. When the Wampanoag leader, Frank James, was informed that his speech was inappropriate and inflammatory for the annual Thanksgiving ceremony in 1970, he refused to read the revised speech presented by the organisers. Instead, he delivered his original speech on Cole's Hill, next to the statue of Ousamequin. This became the first National Day of Mourning, which continues today in Plymouth, Massachusetts, on the same day as Thanksgiving. The action embraced by the American Indian Movement sparked a national trend for tribes to observe a National Day of Mourning instead of the Thanksgiving holiday.

8 Winslow, E. 1622. Mourt's Relation: A Journal of the Pilgrims at Plymouth
10 https://www.presidency.ucsb.edu/documents/proclamation-3560-thanksgiving-day-1963 Accessed by M W Newbury 19/2/2020

CHAPTER TWELVE _____

The Legacy of the Pilgrims

Sadly, the very first settlers who moved to Virginia did unspeakably barbaric things to the indigenous population. However, the *Mayflower* and the three ships that followed them under the same leadership, can be noted for the respectful and tolerant way they interacted with the Wampanoag Indians. Aware that the settlers in Jamestown had violently stolen land from the Native Americans, John Robinson, (who coordinated the plans to settle in America from Holland) was insistent that the Pilgrims should adopt a more ethical approach. He put in writing that land and goods should be bought and not stolen from the Native Americans.

In 1630, 1,000 Puritans arrived under Governor John Winthrup, who established Boston as the capital of the Massachusetts Bay Company and the biggest colony in the area. Tensions between these new colonists and the Native American people grew, while the new arrivals brought yet more diseases. Smallpox ravaged the communities still recovering from the Great Dying, while violence between the factions increased. Conflicts like the Pequot War which took place between 1636 and 1638 led to Native Americans in the region becoming a minority in their own lands.

The peace agreement between the Wampanoag and the Plymouth colony would eventually be shattered by King Philip's War in 1675. When Ousamequin died in 1662, his son and heir, Metacom, no longer saw value in the alliance, with trade agreements being broken and the colonies expanding at an aggressive speed. Tensions reached breaking point, when the colonists demanded the peace agreement should mean the Wampanoag hand over any guns. Tensions soon spilled over into violence and Metacom (known as King Philip by the English) led an uprising of the Wampanoag, Nipmuck, Pocumtuck and Narragansett tribes.

King Philip's War (or the First American War) saw the colonial leaders join forces with their allies, the Mohegans and Mohawks in a conflict that lasted 14 months and raged across Rhode Island, Connecticut and Massachusetts and later spread to Maine and New Hampshire. In proportion to population, the war is considered to be the deadliest in American history and the single greatest disaster of 17th century New England. By the end of the war, more than 600 colonists had died, around 1,200 homes had been burned and 12 of the 90 new settlements destroyed.

The losses were far worse for Native Americans. Out of the 20,000 inhabitants of New England, an estimated 2,000 were killed, another 3,000 had died of sickness and starvation, around 1,000 were captured and sold into slavery and an estimated 2,000 fled to join the Iroquois in the west and Abenaki in the north. This means that between 60 and 80 percent of the native population were lost.[11]

Compared to the Puritans, the Pilgrims of Plymouth failed to achieve lasting economic success and in the early 1630s the likes of Brewster, Winslow and Standish had left to form their own communities. The cost of fighting King Philip's War further damaged the Plymouth colony's finances and less than a decade after the war, King James II appointed a governor to rule over New England. In 1692, less than 75 years after the first landings by the Pilgrim Fathers, Plymouth was absorbed into the larger entity of Massachusetts.

As part of the Mayflower 400 commemorations in 2020, the organisers were keen that the story of the Pilgrims would not be told without the perspective of the indigenous people included. History books are now being rewritten as the devastating impact of colonisation on the Wampanoag people is assessed and published for the first time. In his book, *Mayflower: A Voyage to War*, Nathaniel Philbrick talks of a ship with a similar name to the *Mayflower*, that was to set sail from the shores of New England some 56 years after the Pilgrim's voyage. Like the *Mayflower*, the *Seaflower* carried a human cargo, but rather than colonists, they were Native American Slaves.

The governor of Plymouth Colony, Josiah Winslow (the son of former *Mayflower* passengers Edward and Susanna Winslow) had provided a certificate bearing his official seal saying that these 180 native men, women and children had joined an uprising against the colony and were being condemned to lifelong slavery. The *Seaflower* was one of several New England vessels bound for the West Indies with native slaves. However, the plantation owners of Barbados and Jamaica had little interest in slaves who had already shown a willingness to revolt. We don't know what happened to the Natives Americans aboard the *Seaflower*, but we do know that the captain of one of the ships was forced to sail all the way to Africa before

11 https://historyofmassachusetts.org/what-was-king-philips-war/

offloading his cargo of slaves. Philbrick points out that that "after 56 years, one people's quest for freedom had ended in the conquest and enslaving of another."[12]

The Wampanoag and the wider Native American Nations became an integral part of the Mayflower 400 commemorations. It was important that their voices weren't lost and their story of survival against the odds was told alongside that of the *Mayflower* Pilgrims. There are between 4000 and 5000 members of the Wampanoag Nation living in New England today. They are made up of three primary groups, the Mashpee, Aquinnah and Manomet who continue to claim their heritage and practice their traditions. They do this through sharing stories, holding ceremonies and social gatherings, celebrating through song and dance, hunting and fishing and keeping the Wampanoag language alive.[13]

MORE INFORMATION
THE MAYFLOWER TRAIL APP

The Mayflower Trail App is a self-guided tour which complements the Pilgrims Trail leaflet and encourages visits to the other Pilgrim related destinations in UK and the Netherlands. Mayflower Self-Guided Tours is an innovative and highly detailed app that turns your mobile device into a personal GPS tour guide of the UK towns, cities and villages connected to the *Mayflower*. You can download the app on your mobile device by searching for 'Mayflower 400' in the App and Play stores.

FURTHER READING

Mayflower: A Voyage to War
Nathaniel Philbrick
Harper Perennial. 2006

The Mayflower: The Families, the Voyage and the Founding of America.
Rebecca Fraser
St. Martin's Press. 2017

They Came for Freedom: The Forgotten, Epic Adventure of the Pilgrims
Jay Milbrandt
Nelson Books. 2017

Mayflower: Beyond the Horizon, Anthology of Young People's Writing
Edited by Amy Potter and Laura Roberts
University of Plymouth Press. 2019

Making Haste from Babylon: The Mayflower Pilgrims and Their World: A New History
Nick Bunker
Vintage First Edition 2011
Of Plymouth Plantation
William Bradford
Dover Publications 2006

One Small Candle: The Story of William Bradford and the Pilgrim Fathers
Evelyn Tidman
CreateSpace Independent Publishing Platform 2013

12 Philbrick, N. 2006. Mayflower: A Voyage to War. Harper Perennial. Preface xv
13 https://www.plimoth.org/learn/just-kids/homework-help/who-are-wampanoag Accessed on 26/2/2020.